Golf
Problems
& Solutions

Essential solutions for
all your golfing woes

Golf
Problems
Essential solutions for all your golfing woes
& Solutions

Edited by Duncan Lennard

A DAVID & CHARLES BOOK
Copyright David & Charles Limited 2009

David & Charles is an F+W Media Inc. company
4700 East Galbraith Road
Cincinnati, OH 45236

First published in the UK in 2009
First published in the US in 2009

Golfer

Source material courtesy of *Today's Golfer* magazine © Bauer Consumer Media

A catalogue record for this book is available from the British Library.

ISBN-13: 978-0-7153-3161-3 flexibound
ISBN-10: 0-7153-3161-2 flexibound

Printed in China by SNP Leefung
for David & Charles
Brunel House   Newton Abbot   Devon

Commissioning Editor: Neil Baber
Editor: Bethany Dymond
Art Editor: Martin Smith
Project Editor: Duncan Lennard
Production Controller: Kelly Smith

Visit our website at www.davidandcharles.co.uk

David & Charles books are available from all good bookshops; alternatively you
can contact our Orderline on 0870 9908222 or write to us at FREEPOST
EX2 110, D&C Direct, Newton Abbot, TQ12 4ZZ (no stamp required UK only);
US customers call 800-289-0963 and Canadian customers call 800-840-5220.

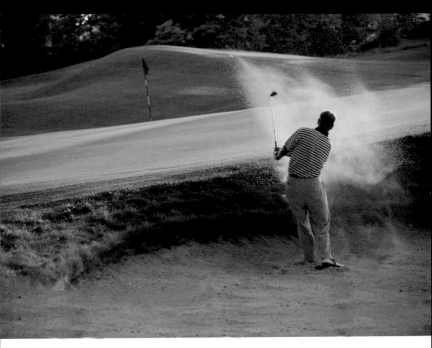

Contents

Introduction

In the heat of battle – and let's face it, even at the driving range – golfers can quite easily lose sight of the fact that every problem has a solution. The true path to golfing enlightenment weaves through more than its fair share of cul-de-sacs: one leads to a stubborn swing flaw; the next to a shot you just can't seem to master. As students of one of the most frustrating games known to man, you can perhaps be forgiven for getting a little lost and despondent now and then.

But for those of you fed up of arriving at dead ends, *Golf Problems & Solutions* is here as your golfing sat-nav. Awash with tips, drills and strategies, each one targeting a specific golfing headache, this book will not just remind you that there are solutions out there; it'll show you how to set about employing them in a clear and methodical way.

A quick flick through the book will show you that the content has been split up into six chapters, from tee to green, allowing you to head straight for the one area of the game that's dishing out the most grief. A seventh chapter deals with those more general but equally pesky technique flaws, like a reverse pivot or an overswing. Each problem is clearly stated at the top of the page, helping you find the relevant solution quickly and easily.

You will soon discover the breadth of the problems identified and solved in these pages. If you want the swing theory and technique, it's here; you can learn the secrets of swing plane on page 28, or find out what causes a flying right elbow – and how to keep it grounded – on page 18.

But as we all know, golf is a lot more than theory. If you want to know how to hole a putt across a bumpy winter green, page 152 holds the key; if you'd like to discover how to hit a high, floating pitch off a downslope, the answer is on page 86. This book covers the practical stuff too, including all those problem shots you thought you couldn't hit. All the common miscues are catered for, from shanks through to fats and thins to the ever-popular slice. There's even a section on Great Escapes, in which you'll learn how to splash out of water and strike a decent backhanded chip shot.

This book's small, manageable format means there's no need for you to wait till you return from the course to use it. Simply slip it in a golf bag pocket and take it to the range or course. It makes a truly useful companion when you feel yourself coming up against a brick wall.

The hints and tips in *Golf Problems & Solutions* come from an established and respected team of professional golf coaches who will be well-known to anyone familiar with *Today's Golfer* magazine. Improving a golfer's technique and score is their day job, and they all excel at it.

Though *Golf Problems & Solutions* is crammed full of indispensable information, the experts can only hope that it answers your specific golfing glitches: the game's challenge is formidable, which is what makes the great shots so pleasurable.

But they are confident it will hit enough bases to take several shots off your score – and restore your belief that your golfing problems *can* be solved.

General Techniques

Golf's most frustrating swing flaws
explained and corrected by a team
of professional coaches

You have trouble controlling the club, and are not hitting the ball as far as you are capable.

 Improve your grip by making sure the club's grip is running through the correct zones of your hands.

Marking the golf glove with a few simple crosses and lines helps to make a correct grip easier to form. Use this step-by-step guide to get it right.

1. Join the crosses

Draw a line of crosses on the inside of your golf glove, so they run diagonally across your fingers. The first cross should be marked on the middle joint of the index finger and the last cross on the fleshy pad at the base of your little finger. The middle two crosses sit on the imaginary line that joins the two crosses together.

A firm grip
Hold the club in your fingers, otherwise all mobility in the hands and wrists will be lost, reducing power and feel.

2. Close the hand

Draw a big lone cross on the fleshy pad at the base of the palm. Rest the grip of the club so that it hides the first four crosses, then close your hand around the handle. Make sure you hide the big lone cross as the hand closes, so that the cross sits directly on top of the handle.

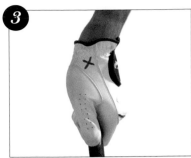

3. Place the thumb

Now place the thumb on top of the handle. It should sit just a fraction to the right of the centre of the grip. Mark a cross on top of your glove, in line with the crease between the thumb and forefinger, to help align your hand with the centre of the handle.

4. Line on the thumb

Draw a straight line along the side of your left thumb to indicate where the lifeline of your right hand should rest. Introduce your right hand to the side of the grip, so that it hides this line, making sure the grip rests in the fingers as the left hand did.

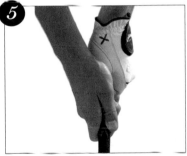

5. Join the hands

The hands work as a unit. Join them either by overlapping the little finger of the right hand, so that it rests in the groove between the index and third finger of your left hand, or by interlocking the hands, letting the little finger of the right hand and the forefinger of the left intertwine.

Your swing feels fine but your shots are flying right of the target.

Aim the club at your target, and not yourself.

One of the biggest myths in golf is to aim your shoulders or your feet at the target. By aiming your shoulders and shoes at the target, your body will get in the way of your swing path. Instead, aim your body parallel to the ball-to-target line.

Fault: closed stance

By aiming your shoulders and feet at the flagstick you have a closed stance and will hit the ball to the right of the target, or have to re-route the club across the target line to strike shots straight. This loopy action usually leads to a slice. Glancing over your shoulder to check your aim will only mislead you into thinking it is correct. Here's how to fix it:

1. Correct alignment

The best way to get your position right is to lay a couple of clubs down on the ground – one pointing at your target for the club to aim at and another parallel to this for your feet to follow. Then all you have to do is square your knees, hips and shoulders to the lower club. Your body will be aiming to the left of the flag.

2. Open stance

Check your aim by rotating your head to the left to look at the target, rather than glancing over your shoulder. This position will probably feel open, or aiming left to you; but accept this is simply because your previous, shut stance felt square.

Your backswing feels restricted, and your swing lacks power. You also have a tendency to hit the ball heavy.

 ## Raise your chin off your chest to achieve a fuller shoulder turn.

One of the worst clichés in golf is that you've got to keep your head down. Do so and you'll end up with poor posture at address, which leads to a shoulder tilt rather than a shoulder turn in the backswing. This cramped, powerless swing causes havoc with your timing – you will probably end up hitting shots fat. Here's how to sort your set-up to free your swing.

No room
Chin on chest leaves no space for your shoulders to turn.

Bad set-up
Focus too much on keeping your head down and your chin will touch your chest. Your shoulders will become rounded, your upper body will be full of tension and that can lead to a steep, powerless swing.

Bad backswing
With the chin touching the chest, the shoulders don't have space to turn so the club gets picked up very steeply with little shoulder rotation. This leads to a steep downward blow and often heavy shots.

Straight spine
Lifting the chin off the chest straightens out the top of the back. A straight spine turns more readily than a bent one, so you'll be able to coil much better from this position.

Good set-up
Focus your eyes on the ball and keep your chin slightly raised so that it is not touching your chest. This straightens the spine angle, giving you a more athletic posture position and a tension-free upper body.

Good backswing
With more room between the chin and chest there is space for the shoulders to pass through freely. This encourages a more powerful backswing turn as there is no tension in your arms.

You have trouble starting the swing smoothly; your swing lacks rhythm.

 Create pre-swing movement to allow you to flow into the takeaway.

Getting your swing off to a smooth start is important, as it sets the tone for a rhythmical, balanced action. Many Tour professionals use a distinctive starting method or trigger. It really doesn't matter what you do. The main thing is to have this trigger and to get your swing on the right track from the start. Try one of these four triggers to get you started.

The trigger: sending a signal
You can use all sorts of triggers to send a signal to your brain, to tell it the swing is about to start. Kicking your right knee in a touch is just one. Try all of the triggers shown here to see which one works best for you.

1. Kick knee in
Golfers who stand like a statue often
struggle to move freely. A simple move
that creates the feeling of readiness
to swing back is to kick your right knee
in towards the target.

2. The waggle
Gripping too tightly creates tension in your
hands and arms and promotes a jerky
action. To remove the tension, waggle the
club back and forth a few times before
you swing.

3. Hover the club
Raise your driver off the ground to hover
behind the ball. By lifting the club you
are free to make a smooth takeaway, and
eliminate any chance of the club snagging
the ground.

4. Brush the grass
Let the sole of your driver gently graze
the tops of the blades of grass in the
takeaway. This smooth movement will
create a feeling of timing and balance
in your swing.

Your arms disconnect from your torso as the backswing unfolds, creating the so-called 'flying right elbow'.

 Keep a constant gap between your arms and body throughout the backswing.

1. Arms hang down freely

Start by getting good posture at address. Bend forwards from the hips, keep your back straight and a slight flex in your knees. Let the arms hang down naturally beneath your shoulders, so your right elbow faces your right hip. Now grip the club, keeping a palm's width gap between your hands and your body.

2. Focus on your turn

Don't let your arms get trapped close to your body as you swing the club away. Starting on this inside path forces you to swing up and across the line in the backswing to compensate. Halfway back, your left shoulder, left hand and clubhead should be in a straight line at hip height, with your right elbow facing the ground.

3. Maintain the triangle

It is easy to allow your arms to overstretch and your elbows to creep away from the body, pushing the club up very high to the top of your backswing. Fight this by feeling that the left shoulder just brushes the underside of your chin as you turn back. At the top, your right elbow should be sitting directly under the shaft of your club.

You sway laterally from side-to-side during the swing, promoting poor striking and inconsistency.

 Wedge a towel under the outside of your right foot to feel how the back leg should resist your backswing turn and support your weight.

One of the most common faults golfers make is to sway from side-to-side in the swing. It robs your swing of consistency, length and control. An effective drill to help eliminate swaying is to swing with a golf towel placed under the side of your right foot. This acts as a wedge and helps you keep your weight on the inside of the right leg and foot during the backswing.

Foot resistor
Wedging a towel under your right foot forces you to keep the resistan on the inside of yc right leg and foot you reach the top.

Side-to-side sway
The sway happens because the hips move to the side rather than turning in the swing. The weight transfers to the outside of the right leg and the right foot rolls to the side or lifts in the backswing.

Your club ends up past parallel at the top of the backswing, an overswing that costs power and control.

Make a conscious decision to take a shorter, more compact backswing.

Rather than storing up power in your backswing, the overswing robs you of coil, effectively destroying that power store. Also, as the club has a long way to return to the ball, your chances of returning it to impact square are greatly reduced, compromising accuracy. Worst of all, the overswing kills the much-needed rhythm and timing to your swing, so you'll lose consistency and distance control will be impossible. Shortening your swing will work wonders with all of the above.

Way beyond parallel
When the club swings beyond parallel you'll lose control and timing. The result is that the coil store in your torso breaks down and the club will return to the ball with less power and less consistency.

Parallel lines
The shaft of the driver should finish parallel to the ground, or just short. When you practise, feel that you only take the club half the distance back. What feels short to you will actually be a three-quarter swing.

You lose your balance during the swing, impeding your ability to create any kind of controlled power.

 Grab a club and focus on three crucial parts of the swing – set-up, top-of-backswing and finish.

Great weight transfer means shifting your weight on to the right side in the backswing and then back to the left side in the through-swing – and, most importantly, making this movement with the body in balance. Improve your shift with these three checkpoints – address, the top, and the finish.

1. Set-up: even balance

Your weight should be evenly distributed between both feet at set-up (see right). Keep the weight slightly forward on the balls of your feet, so you feel balanced and ready to swing. This will encourage an athletic posture, getting you in great shape, poised and ready to fire. The best way to practise getting into a great address is to imagine you are standing on the edge of a diving board, ready to jump in.

Practise barefoot
A great way to get great footwork in the swing is to practise swinging barefoot. This will give you a much better awareness and feel for the weight distribution in your feet.

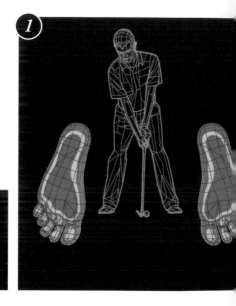

2. At the top: shift weight to the right

As you swing back, your weight should start shifting gradually on to your right side. By the top of the backswing the majority of weight should have moved on to your right side; just 20 per cent is on the left foot, which braces the upper body turn. You should feel the majority of this weight resisting against the inside of your left golf shoe.

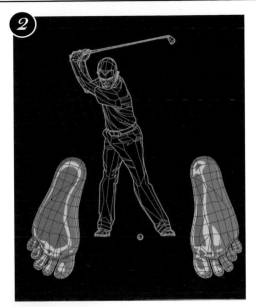

3. Finish: transfer weight through

The weight should gradually shift back on to the left side, to balance out the distribution of weight in your feet as you hit the ball, and then continue to push through on to the left side as you complete the swing. The followthrough position should be 80 per cent of weight on your left side and just 20 per cent of weight on the right foot.

Your weight moves forward on the backswing and back on the way through – the classic reverse pivot.

 Focus on your lower body; control your knee movement for a better weight shift.

A big club golfer problem is to point the left knee at the ball. It leaves too much weight on the left side at address and, as the swing begins, the knee buckles under the pressure, dipping forwards and causing the right knee to straighten out to compensate. This classic fault is called the reverse pivot and leads to no end of swing errors, the most typical being a slice. Keeping both knees evenly flexed is the solution to this weight imbalance. Follow these four steps to fix it.

Poor pivot
If your left knee shifts down and forwards towards the ground, you have a typical reverse pivot, and need to work on keeping your knees level and evenly flexed throughout your swing.

Common fault
If your left knee over flexes, your right knee will be forced to straighten in the backswing to compensate for the excess movement.

1. Knees flex out
Good set up
Flex both knees so they are pointing over the corresponding toes. As you swing back, focus on feeling the resistance on the inside of your left leg. This should prevent the knee dipping forwards towards the ground.

2. Shaft your problems
Even flex
To help you train to keep the left knee flexed and pointing over your left toe, try this drill. Wedge a mid-iron into the ground so that it points at a 45-degree angle across your legs. Now swing back and make sure the knee doesn't push the shaft forwards.

Flex and face forward
As you swing to the top, your left knee should stay flexed and facing forwards. If it pushes the shaft towards the ground, you are not keeping the resistance.

3. Right elbow to right knee
Pull down
The reverse pivot generally causes an over-the-top downswing. To stop this, feel your right elbow stay close to the right side as you start the downswing. Pulling the arms down together towards the right hip, and not towards the ball, should ensure your downswing starts on the correct path.

4. Keep your balance
Finish pose
By keeping your knee flex constant, you should feel a lot more balanced throughout the swing. Your aim is to finish facing the target with all your weight on the left foot and the club over your shoulders.

Your arms collapse on the way back, robbing the swing of width and force.

Picture your swing as a circle, and retain width between your right arm and shoulder as you swing to the top.

Right elbow buckles

Golfers looking for extra turn can easily bend their right elbow excessively in the backswing in order to try and maximize their shoulder rotation.

This can cause the club to be pulled on an extreme inside path around the torso, which causes the arms to feel disconnected from the body. From here, the club usually gets cast back over the top, leading to an out-to-in pass through impact with arms buckling. That poor arm motion causes the left arm to collapse in close to the body in the through-swing. The result is a weak slice out to the right.

Collapsing elbow
Golfers wanting a big backswing turn can let their right elbow collapse. It leads to a narrow arc and a weak fade.

Maintain set-up width

Your swing should follow a circular path around your body. In order to keep the circle in your swing, you must ensure you keep your hands a constant distance from the body throughout.

Start by setting up to the ball. Grip the club so your hands hang about a palm's width away from the body. Then concentrate on keeping the same width between the right hand and right shoulder as you swing to the top of your backswing. Look to maintain this width as the club strikes the ball and the arms extend through towards the target to complete the finish. You should find your shots have more control … and with an improved backswing turn your power will be greater too.

Consistent spacing
At set-up, focus on the gap between your right hand and shoulder. Retain that width to the top of the backswing.

Your swing is either overly upright or flat, causing loss of accuracy and general inconsistency.

 You must improve your swing plane – with help from a cardboard box.

Swinging on plane is the key to hitting shots longer and straighter with consistency. You can cut a cardboard box in half and use it as a simple guide to check swing plane positions. Try these simple steps at home.

Square to the target
Notice how the shoulders are square to the target at this point, mirroring the target line on the ground. The upper body has not over-rotated and pulled the club on the inside.

Set the position
When you practise, rehearse this backswing move and set the club in the perfect position halfway back, so the shaft is parallel to the target line and the clubface is square, pointing away from you.

1. Avoid starting inside the line
Common fault

The club has been taken away too far on the inside. From this position the club is likely to remain open at the top of the swing and then, coming back down into the ball, a slice left to right will be hit.

2. On plane at the top
Set the position

The ideal position at the top sees the club finishing just short of parallel, pointing towards the target. From here feel your left side initiate the downswing. Shift your hips towards the target, then let your arms pull the club back down towards the ball on the backswing path.

3. Return to square
Time the release

If you follow the same swing path up and down, the club's face should return to impact square to your target. By using the box as a guideline, you can check you release the club through impact correctly, shaft parallel to the target line halfway into the through-swing.

4. Stay connected through
Reach the finish

If you don't continue to swing the club through on the correct plane, following the inward curve of the imaginary oval arc, then your swing path will alter the ball flight direction. Keep the arms close to your body. They should stay connected in the same way they did in the backswing.

The clubface comes in hooded to the ball, causing a vicious pull-hook.

 Weaken your grip to help the clubface rotate with your body turn.

Closed clubface

Golfers who duck hook shots left often do so because they start with a very strong grip, with three or more knuckles on their left hand showing. As the hands will always naturally return to a neutral position at impact, the clubface is shut as you strike the ball. An in-to-in swing path will exaggerate the fault and cause the nasty pull-hook that hounds many games.

Neutralize your grip

Start by gripping the club correctly, so that only two knuckles of your left hand are showing. From this position, the club should rotate in tune with your body turn.

With a weaker grip, the toe will point slightly down to the ground halfway back. This will eliminate the need for excessive hand action and help you to naturally return your club to square at impact.

Hooker's swing
In a typical hooker's swing the club gets taken away on an inside path, the face over-rotating to compensate.

Loosened grip
With a weaker grip, the club will be slightly closed halfway back. This stops the need to roll the face shut.

Your game lacks general control and consistency.

Your legs are the foundation of the golf swing. Follow these three steps to give your action more stability.

Understanding how to control your legs during the swing is fundamental to hitting shots with more power and greater accuracy. There are three steps to great leg action:

1. Set-up

Your legs should be flexed with athletic poise when you address the ball. Try to keep your knees pressed slightly apart, to give you a little bit of resistance in the legs without feeling tense.

2. Backswing

As you swing back, feel the resistance on the inside of your left leg and right thigh. Focus on keeping the same distance between your knees that you started with at address.

3. Impact

Your upper and lower body should be synchronized, so that you drive your right knee towards the target in time with your right arm – they should be in line at impact. This action will guarantee a solid ball strike.

From the Tee

Tips and drills created to fire power
and accuracy into your tee game
– and get the hole off to a great start.

Your tee game lacks the power to take on long, modern courses.

 Create swing force by adding width and building lower-body resistance.

Gone are the days when accuracy and finesse ruled. Today's game is a power game, and if you're short off the tee you're at a serious disadvantage. The good news is you don't need to be built like the Incredible Hulk to hit the ball further. Power is all about great timing. Get it right and you can gain upwards of 20 yards off the tee. Swing width and clubhead speed are the two essential keys to distance, and a few simple swing moves can generate serious power in even the smallest players. Here are four ways you can add yards to your drives … without gaining an ounce of muscle.

Set the L-shape position
Your halfway back checkpoint is that your forearms and club form an L-shape. The feeling of soft wrists will help you to set this correct shape, without any undue resistance to your backswing turn.

Don't overdo width
Many golfers get confused when they hear the word 'width' and extend the club straight out to the side of their body. This position severely restricts turn.

No wrist hinge
This is a classic power-robbing fault, which sees the club pointing too far away from you.

Ball in sight
You should be able to see at least half the ball above the top of the clubhead when hovering next to the ball at address.

1. Build a powerful platform
Dynamic address

The first step to a powerful golf swing is to build a strong base around which to swing. That means widening your stance a touch more than usual, so your feet are wider apart than your shoulders. Turn your toes out a little, to give you a nice stable footing, and flex your knees to point slightly outwards. Tee the ball high and hover your driver for a smoother takeaway. The high tee height promotes a higher launch angle, which means your ball will travel further in the air, adding distance to your drives.

Body uncoils
Make sure your upper body and lower body turn together into impact.

Use the knee
Shift your weight on to your right side by driving your right knee through.

2. Into impact: right heel raised
Time the move

The most powerful golf swings are those where the lower body and upper body uncoil in unison into impact. This perfect timing ensures that maximum power is unloaded into the ball. The right heel should raise as you transfer your weight on to the left side into impact. Allow the right knee to move diagonally across towards the target as you strike the ball. By doing this, your hips keep rotating and weight is transferred correctly from one side to the other.

Square the clubface
If the right heel stays glued to the floor, the hands are forced to over work to square the clubface, often causing a snap hook.

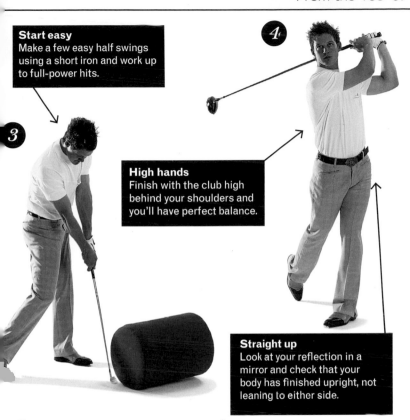

Start easy
Make a few easy half swings using a short iron and work up to full-power hits.

3

High hands
Finish with the club high behind your shoulders and you'll have perfect balance.

4

Straight up
Look at your reflection in a mirror and check that your body has finished upright, not leaning to either side.

3. Power strike: hit it hard
Use a bag to build aggression

If you want to send the ball soaring, you have to hit it hard. That doesn't mean thrashing with no control; it means a well-timed, powerful strike. Grab a large bean bag or invest in an impact bag, and practise making full-power strikes. This will keep your left side firm coming into impact and prevents any flicking of the wrists.

4. Finish: stay balanced
Left-sided, upright finish

Powerful players always finish in perfect balance, facing the target. The golden rule is to hit the ball as hard as you like as long as you can reach this stable finish position, with your weight on the left side and the body upright. Make sure you are not leaning over to one side, because you could topple over and hit shots off-line.

Your lower body will not support a wide, powerful swing, causing you to lose coil.

 Set your knees pointing out at address, and maintain the gap between them as you turn.

Think of the swing as being built from the base up, starting with the set-up. Building a solid base around which to turn is an essential part of generating power in your swing. The knees are important tools in that process. Flex them correctly and you'll have no problem making the swing moves that are needed to generate power and consistency off the tee. However, allow them to collapse and you'll lose all the coil and torque in your backswing turn, robbing you of power as you strike the ball. Get these three key moves right:

1. Strong address

See how the knees are pointing outwards at address. This gives a good strong base around which to turn. It's the same in many other sports. Imagine you are a boxer: you would plant your legs wide and steady before delivering your blow.

2. Keep the width constant

As you swing back, focus on keeping the width consistent between your flexed knees. Don't allow your left knee to collapse across towards your right knee, as you'll lose the coil and power.

3. Followthrough

If you've successfully built a strong base and maintained this in the backswing, the strike and followthrough should come naturally. Keep the left knee flex strong and drive your right knee and right side across into the ball.

Your swing is sequenced poorly, robbing your driving of timing, power and consistency.

 Add tempo to your action by following these four steps.

The golf swing is such a complex movement that one bad move can throw everything out of sync. But to get things in the right order, and generate power, follow this four-step sequence.

Tempo is key
Great timing is critical to generating power. The upper and lower body must uncoil in unison to deliver clubhead speed.

Power platform – keep a stable base
A powerful swing starts with a powerful stance. Plant your feet wide apart at address to reduce your leg action and increase resistance against the body turn.

1. Feel the resistance

To generate greater torque you must keep your leg action 'quiet', to help build resistance in your swing. To do this, maintain the same distance between the knees in the backswing.

2. Keep good angles

A loss of posture is the biggest killer of power in the swing. Try to maintain the spine angle, and keep your right knee flexed as you swing to the top and then back to the ball.

3. Let the club lag

Watch any big-hitting Tour pro and you'll see that the wrists stay hinged and don't release the club into impact until the last moment. Copy this lag to increase clubhead speed.

4. Hit the wall

The upper and lower body must uncoil in unison. Feel the resistance on your left side at impact, like you are hitting a wall, keeping your head and chest behind the ball.

You are not finding enough fairways, and it's costing you on the scorecard.

 Pay more attention to club selection and course management and, above all, tailor your ambition to your ability.

Aim away from trouble
When you're faced with a tough tee shot, you really have to pay attention to the hazards ahead. It's tempting to have a bash with the driver no matter what, but there's a lot at stake. You only need to pull it slightly and your ball will be bouncing on the rocks.

Par-4s are often the toughest holes on the golf course. You know you have to find the fairway off the tee to give yourself a chance of getting to the green, but at the same time there's so much trouble to contend with that the smallest mishit will be punished badly.

When faced with a daunting tee shot, don't automatically go for the driver and 'hit and hope'. There could be an easier alternative that will still allow you to have a crack at that green, so that you can walk away with a par or, at worst, a bogey on your scorecard.

Break 80
This daunting tee shot should be as easy as shelling peas. Driving is your strength, and you hit the ball long and straight. Time to use your advantage by smashing the ball down the right side of the fairway, to set up a short approach shot into the green.

Break 100
Inconsistency is your Achilles heel. Faced with a tough tee shot, you simply can't afford to hit and hope – you need to find the fairway. The safest option is to play a lofted long iron and aim for the right side of the fairway. Your margin for error is larger here.

Break 90
Driving isn't your strongest suit. You can hit the ball miles, but not always in the right direction. A lofted fairway wood is your best friend – the shorter shaft means less can go wrong, so your bad shots won't be as destructive and finding the fairway is easier.

Break 100: use the tee
To make this shot easier, tee the ball up a little higher so you can clip it cleanly. Keep your grip pressure light. To find the right grip pressure, hold your club out in front of you, at 45 degrees to your body, and bounce it up and down in your hands – this is about the right force to use.

Break 100: aim right
Good alignment is the single most important factor for you to concentrate on. Pick out a target on the safe side of the fairway in the distance. Now look from behind the ball and use a spot on the ground in line with the target you've identified as an alignment aid. Aim your club at this and aim your feet parallel to this line. As a rule, always sort the clubface aim first, and then set your body up square to it.

Break 90: make life easier

There's no need to make this tee shot harder than necessary. Using a 3-wood, instead of a driver, will ensure you are more accurate. Keep the club low to the ground in the takeaway (**1**) and make a full shoulder turn so that your back faces the target (**2**).

Break 80: time to attack

You want to hit the drive of your life – here's how to do it. Set up so your hips are tilted, pushing your spine angle slightly behind the ball (**1**). Load your weight on to the right in the backswing, turning so the left shoulder is above the right kneecap, like a discus player (**2**).

You keep topping the ball off the tee.

 Stick a tee peg into the butt of your driver and use it as a reference to shallow your swing.

Most topped shots are caused by swing path problems. To fix this fault you must bring the club down on an inside path.

Using a tee peg

To ensure you strike the base of the ball and not the top, pop a tee peg into the hole in the butt end of your grip. Swing to the top, then, as you swing down, check to see where the peg is pointing. It should be pointing at the back of your ball. Anywhere beyond or above your ball and your shoulders have overtaken the arms, and you'll hit down on top of the ball. This will shallow your swing path to help you sweep shots away.

Tee peg laser check
Imagine a laser light is shining out of the end of your tee peg in the grip. The peg's light should point at the back of your golf ball.

The ball shoots upwards off the crown of the driver, the dreaded skied shot.

 Alter weight distribution at set-up.

Set-up fault: leaning towards the ball
This places too much weight on the left foot, opens the body and leads to a steep swing with a lack of weight transfer. It causes you to hit down sharply into the ball, skying it off the top of the driver.

Shift the weight: drop your right shoulder
Tilt your upper body so that your right shoulder sits lower than your left. This strong set-up position encourages you to strike the ball on an upward, rather than a downward, swing path.

You just can't stop hitting chronic slices off the tee.

 Learn how to rotate your forearms correctly through impact.

Before impact

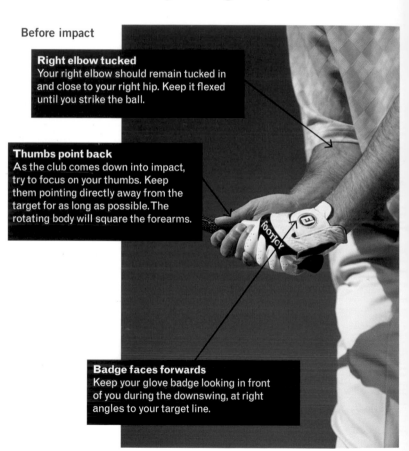

Right elbow tucked
Your right elbow should remain tucked in and close to your right hip. Keep it flexed until you strike the ball.

Thumbs point back
As the club comes down into impact, try to focus on your thumbs. Keep them pointing directly away from the target for as long as possible. The rotating body will square the forearms.

Badge faces forwards
Keep your glove badge looking in front of you during the downswing, at right angles to your target line.

Most club golfers are aware that the clubface's aim pretty much follows the back of the left hand and the palm of the right. Because of this link, many attempt to hit straight by keeping their glove badge looking down the target line for as long as possible either side of the ball – a misguided attempt to hold the face square. Don't! This stops your arms working with your rotating body and leads to a weak, dead-wristed and blocky action, usually sending the ball way right. Instead, accept the fact the clubface should be constantly rotating like a swing door, passing through a square position not swinging to one.

Through the ball

Forearms touch
In fact, they might not quite; but it's a great thought to help develop the correct rotating movement through the ball.

Thumbs up
With good forearm rotation your hands will turn over as you strike the ball and the thumbs will point up towards the sky.

Lower hand faces forwards
Coming into the ball, the back of your glove hand faced out in front of you; in this mirror image, the palm of your glove hand faces out in front of you.

You hit the ball OK on the range, but your slice shows up on the course.

Here are three quick drills you can try on the course that will help you regain the right feelings.

Split the hands
Grip with an inch between them. This split grip promotes forearm rotation, which helps you square up the clubface.

Lift your left heel
Lifting the left heel pushes your body's centre of gravity back behind the ball and allows your arms to swing the club to the ball undisturbed.

Swing a flag
Swinging a six-foot pole widens your swing arc, making it almost impossible to swing out-to-in. Let the flag just swish the ground as you swing back and forth. Feel it flatten your action.

You're having trouble finding your driver's sweet-spot.

 Address the ball out of the toe.

When the ball is teed up high you must address it out of the toe. At impact, the club is off the ground. Hold the club above the ground in your impact position, then let the clubhead drop to the ground. You will see the clubhead move closer to your feet and the ball lines up with its toe. By addressing the ball out of the toe, your driver will strike the ball out of the centre by the time it returns to impact, and your drives will fly longer and straighter.

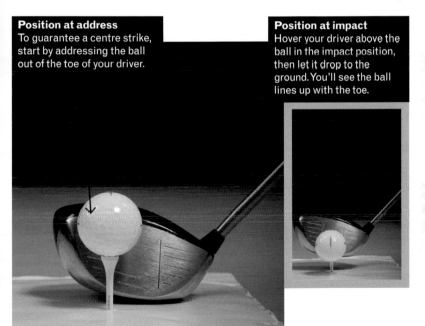

Position at address
To guarantee a centre strike, start by addressing the ball out of the toe of your driver.

Position at impact
Hover your driver above the ball in the impact position, then let it drop to the ground. You'll see the ball lines up with the toe.

From the Fairway

These green-hitting keys cover all on-course scenarios ... and will see you putting for birdie more often

Your iron shots lack punch and penetration, and do not apply backspin to the ball.

 Follow these four simple steps to develop a ball–turf connection.

The ideal iron strike sees the famous ball–turf connection. The clubface swings into the ball on a slight downward arc, 'trapping' the ball against the ground before biting into the turf. This downward strike eliminates the likelihood of a fat shot and applies backspin, which holds the ball straight, lets it climb and sees it settle quickly on landing. But how should you be achieving it? Here are four ball–turf basics guaranteed to boost ball striking.

2. Set the wrists
Single hand swing drill
Wrist hinge promotes a downward strike. Feel the right move by placing your right hand under the left, as shown. Swing back; the club hinges, creating this L-shape.

1. Hands forward
Focus on your set-up
The ball–turf strike needs a downward strike. Use your set-up to promote this; play the ball in the middle of your stance and look for a left arm/clubshaft straight line.

4. Picture the finish
Swing with balance
Swing to a predetermined finish and you can influence your action for the better. So picture a finish where your head ends up over your left foot – a position that means good balance and weight transfer on to the front foot.

3. Right heel rises
Weight shifts forwards
You'll find a downward, squeezing strike much more easily when your weight is ahead of the ball at impact. Make it happen by feeling your right heel rise as the club approaches the ball.

You keep missing greens to the right.

 Improve your understanding of a slice to swing more down the line.

Backswing
The club is 'laid off' at the top, which means the shaft aims left of the target.

Downswing
The upper body gets ahead of the hands and arms on the way down.

Impact
The club cuts across the target line as it strikes the ball.

Imagine a line from the target running through your ball and the clubface. Slicers attack the ball from outside this line, swinging left of the target. The clubface opens (aims right) to compensate as it cuts across the target line. You can get away with it using a lofted club, but with a driver it'll will catch you out every time. The first step to ditching the slice is to gain the ability to picture how an on-line swing should look. Here are the dos and don'ts:

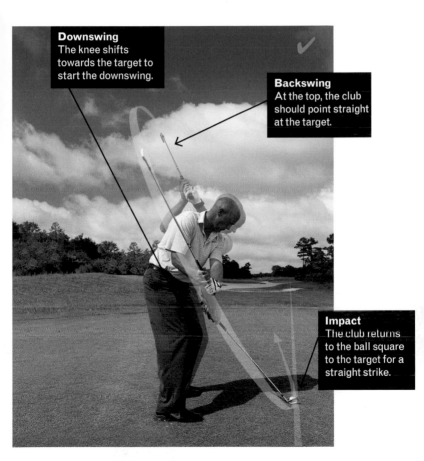

Downswing
The knee shifts towards the target to start the downswing.

Backswing
At the top, the club should point straight at the target.

Impact
The club returns to the ball square to the target for a straight strike.

You've found the fairway but have a tree between your ball and the green.

 Pick the right option – over, under or around – for your standard of play.

The Low Shot

BREAK 100

The play
Playing to the side will hardly advance the ball, while trying to go over is risky business. Your safest, and simplest, option is to play a low runner below the branches.

The club
Use a 4- or 5-iron. You need the ball to fly somewhere between head height and the ground; the limited loft on these clubs will help you to achieve that.

Down under
Make a short, punchy swing, knocking a firm-wristed shot below the branches.

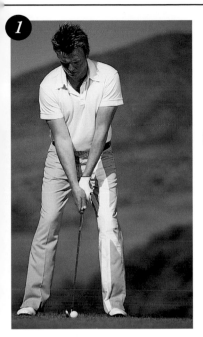

1. Grip down

You need to make a short swing and it's not easy to control the clubface with a longish iron. So shorten it – grip down the club an inch or so. Play the ball centrally in your stance to encourage a slightly downward strike that will help you to keep the ball low.

2. Short is sweet

This shot is about control, not distance, so swing back no further than three-quarter length. Make a hand-and-arm movement, with no great weight shift. Simply try to find this L-shaped position, formed between your left arm and the clubshaft.

3. Firm left wrist

If you let your wrists go loose they will flap loft into the clubface, causing the ball to soar into the branches. Instead, keep them quiet through the hitting zone: keep your through-swing short and finish the swing with your left arm and clubshaft forming a line.

The High Shot

BREAK 90

The play

At your level, getting the ball into the air should not be a problem. The percentage shot for you is to take the tree out of play by going over it.

The club

Naturally this will depend on the height of the tree, but don't mess with the top branches – if you think you can clear it with an 8-iron, pick a 9.

Sweep it away

Play the ball forwards, off your left instep. Keep the club low to the ground early on to set up a sweeping arc and promote a wide angle of attack.

Up and over

Stop your weight jumping forwards by keeping your back heel low to the ground.

Weight 50-50

On most shots your weight shifts into your front side through the ball. But here, try to hold it even. Keep your right heel grounded and your head steady.

A curve ball
Use a 7-iron, get your set-up spot on, then swing in steep to create a left-to-right fade.

Pick a line
Picture the path you need the ball to start on. Set-up square to it. Play the ball forward to encourage an out-to-in swing path. The clubface aims at the green.

Steep shaft
Use an upright backswing. Use plenty of wrist hinge and feel the shaft standing vertically when your left arm is parallel to the ground.

Hit a Fade
BREAK 80

The play
It you want to shoot low, you need to bend the ball to the green. Let the branches and terrain dictate the shot. This scenario calls for a left-to-right fade.

The club
Use about a 7-iron. You need sidespin, and the straighter the face, the easier that will be. If the shot is short, use a longer club and restrict your swing.

Right palm under grip
It's vital the clubface does not turn over. Finish the swing with your right palm under the grip and your glove badge facing the sky.

You've found the fairway but your ball has wound up on a steep slope.

 Set-up for a swing that flows with the gradient and does not try to fight it.

Uphill battle

1. Uphill stance
Lean with the slope. Your shoulders should be parallel to the ground, your weight favouring your right side, and the ball a fraction forwards in your stance.

2. Aim right to offset draw
This lie tends to restrict body motion, resulting in the arms taking over and the clubface rotating closed. Allow for this by aiming a little right.

3. Shorten the finish
The upslope will promote a right-to-left draw. Gain control by keeping your arm swing shorter in the followthrough, promoting a three-quarter swing.

Downhill struggle

1. Fit into the slope

Again, make sure you lean with the slope, keeping your shoulders parallel to the ground. Your weight should favour your left side. Move the ball back a fraction in your stance to ensure you catch it cleanly.

2. Strike down the slope

A downhill slope promotes a lower flight. Allow for this by taking a club with more loft than you would normally choose. Don't be tempted into trying to help the ball up in the air – let the clubface do that for you.

3. Chase it forwards

Don't worry if you end up losing your balance as you sweep the ball away. This can't be helped on a severe slope. Just make sure you transfer your weight fully on to your left side as you swing through.

64

The ball comes out off the shank of the club – where the shaft meets the head – shooting the ball at right-angles across the fairway.

 Stabilize your set-up to promote a better backswing path.

The shank occurs because the club gets delivered to the ball from an extreme inside-to-outside path, causing the heel of the club to strike the ball. The origin of this problem is often a sloppy set-up position, which leads to a poor swing path. With the weight too far forwards on your toes at address, the body will collapse forwards in the backswing. As the club gets taken away the right leg straightens, rather than maintaining its flex, and the club gets dragged on an inside path behind the body. It then returns to the ball on the same extreme path.

A sure sign of shank
When the right leg straightens it forces the body to dip forwards towards the ball. The club then gets dragged away on an extreme inside path behind your body.

Centre your weight

To stop shanking shots work on weight distribution at address. Rock your weight back and forth until you can settle with it centrally on the balls of your feet. A stable address position helps you to take the club away on perfect plane.

Better balance and poise
Make sure you maintain the posture angles you establish at address throughout the swing. Do not let your body collapse forwards towards the ball.

Settle weight evenly
To find perfect balance try rocking your weight back and forth in your shoes. You should be able to feel the happy-medium point, with the majority of weight on the balls of your feet.

Your ball is lying in an old divot.

Move the ball back in your stance and hit down sharply.

You've hit a perfect shot straight down the middle of the fairway. To your disgust, when you reach your ball you find it nestled in a nasty deep divot. The rules say you have to play the ball as it lies, and you must play by the book. Follow these five steps:

1. Take control
Take one extra club than normal and choke down the grip a touch for added control.

2. Ball back
Move the ball back in your stance a few inches. This will help you pick the club up steeper and hit down sharper, to ensure crisp contact with the ball.

3. Weight forwards
Your weight should favour the front foot rather than the back. This will encourage the clubhead to meet the ball before it can make contact with the ground.

4. Hand position
Concentrate on making sure your hands stay ahead of the clubhead as you strike the ball.

5. Drill down
The club should drill into the divot, creating another divot within the divot.

Divot strategy
Strike down steeply into the back
of the ball before the divot.

You keep thinning your iron shots, as revealed by telltale scuffs on the ball.

 Stop trying to help the ball up; get your weight forwards to promote a downward strike.

Before you chuck those old marked balls away, take a closer look at those scuff marks. If your ball has a clear smiley face-shaped cut mark, then this is a telltale sign that you are not striking the ball correctly. Great ball strikers crunch the base of the ball, where it rests on the turf. Poor ball strikers catch it halfway up the ball, sending their shots thinning low to the ground. Here's a quick explanation of why it happens, and how to make your ball striking pure.

What's the cause?
The club strikes halfway up the ball, leaving a nasty scuff mark and sending the shot scudding off low to the ground.

Why does it happen?
Usually, through trying to 'help' the ball up. It leaves weight on the right side and the hands flick at the ball.

How to avoid it
You need to get the club to strike the base of the ball, crunching it off the turf with a punchy control and precision.

What you must do
Trust the loft on the clubface to send the ball up; and shift weight forwards for a descending blow.

You habitually strike the ground before the ball from the fairway.

 Encourage a little head movement and weight transfer – a static head position can cause the duff.

One of the most common swing myths in golf is that your head has to stay still to strike the ball well. This is nonsense and will lead to a catalogue of bad shots, including the fat – catching the ground heavy before the ball. Fortunately, the solutions are simple.

Common myth
If your head stays rock still on the way back, your body is forced to dip to the ball in the downswing, bringing the club into the turf on an overly steep angle.

Sweep it away
Training your body to strike the ball cleanly is easy by learning a more sweeping action. Teeing the ball up high will help you to develop that feel.

1. Fault: body dips
Statue still

If your head stays still, the body will lose height in the downswing, driving the club into the ground. To counter this, try swinging in front of a mirror; focus on keeping the height in your upper body throughout. You can even draw a line on the mirror, under your set-up chin position, to monitor your head height.

Fix: tee it high
Clip it cleanly

Tea a ball up on a high tee peg, with the peg only just pushed into the ground. Now hover a mid-iron (7-iron or equivalent) behind. Your goal is to make a full swing, clipping the ball away off the top of the tee peg, leaving the peg in the ground.

2. Fault: no weight transfer
Hands flip up

Here, with the head focused down at the ball, the right side hasn't moved and the weight hasn't transferred to the left. The hands are forced to work harder to square the club. Better weight transfer will help the club travel through, maintaining the correct loft for the shot.

Fix: picture-perfect finish
Look ahead

Your aim should be to followthrough towards your target, transferring your weight fully on to the left side of your body, and finishing in a picture-perfect pose facing your target. The right foot up on the toe is a good sign that the weight has moved forwards.

You suffer from poor ball flight with fairway woods.

 Develop a wide, sweeping action, starting with a smooth takeaway.

The correct swing arc for a fairway wood is a rounded action, similar to that of a baseball pitcher. You need a slow, smooth takeaway to set the tone for the correct swing arc. You also need immaculate rhythm to ensure the club does the work for you. There are three simple drills you can use to make these skills become second nature. Here's how they work.

1. Push the ball away

The ideal takeaway for a fairway wood sees the clubhead stay low to the ground as your shoulders turn. Try placing a ball directly behind your clubhead at set-up: as you start the takeaway, push the ball back.

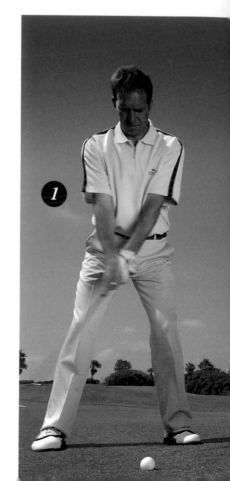

2. Pull your rear foot back

The swing fairway wood is more rounded. To train your muscles to do this, address the ball square to the target ... then pull your right foot back a couple of inches. This gives the hips more room to turn.

3. Upside-down club

Here's a drill to hone smooth tempo: turn the club upside down, gripping beneath the clubhead. Swing the club back and forth. You'll feel the clubhead weight more as the lighter grip end moves more easily.

You still have a long way to go – and it's into the wind.

 Take the driver – and trust the loft on the face to get the ball airborne.

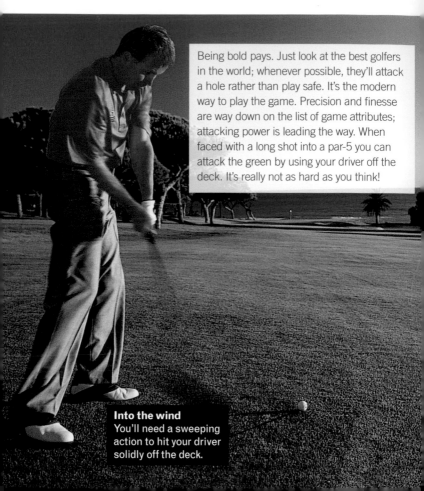

Being bold pays. Just look at the best golfers in the world; whenever possible, they'll attack a hole rather than play safe. It's the modern way to play the game. Precision and finesse are way down on the list of game attributes; attacking power is leading the way. When faced with a long shot into a par-5 you can attack the green by using your driver off the deck. It's really not as hard as you think!

Into the wind
You'll need a sweeping action to hit your driver solidly off the deck.

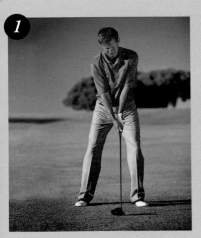

1. Tweak your set-up

Start by positioning the ball as you would for a normal tee shot – just inside your left heel. Keep your hands level with the club. Don't push them ahead, because this will deloft the club and cause you to top the shot. Always remember that with this shot you're looking to hit the ball forwards not upwards or downwards.

2. Sweeping swing arc

You need a sweeping action to play this shot well. Let the clubhead graze the top of the grass as it moves away from the ball and swing a little more around your body like a baseball pitcher. Let your right elbow drop into your side on the way down – the club will lag on the inside so you attack the ball from a shallow angle.

Why drivers work

Most drivers have at least nine degrees of loft, so there's really no reason why the ball can't get airborne off the deck just as it does with a 3-wood. There's simply no need to tee the ball up high and let it fly. Don't try to help your shots into the air; you just have to trust the club's loft to do the work for you.

100 Yards and In

Whatever your short game malaise, these tips and drills will see you enter the scoring zone with confidence

Busy hands compromise distance control on pitch shots.

 Limit weight shift and retain your spine angle to quieten your hands.

The world's best pitchers clip the ball pin-high time and again because they keep the loft on the club's face constant throughout the swing. Problems arise when an action adds loft to, or takes it from, the face. The first key to beating this is keeping your action simple; the second is to keep your hands quiet. These four steps will improve your pitching distance control.

Under control
Keeping the clubhead square throughout your swing means you will always use the same amount of loft, which will boost your levels of consistency.

Stand still
Avoiding too much weight shift will help you to get a crisp contact with the ball; maintaining your spine angle will help you retain the club's loft.

1. Favour your left side

A club dangling from your chest should hang slightly forwards of your ball. This stops any great weight shift, making your action more about control than power.

2. Watch your wrists

Don't be afraid to make a full wrist set. This keeps your swing compact and controlled, and helps avoid the wide swing arc that can cause you to shift weight.

3. The right angle

Maintain your set-up spine angle as you start down. Straighten up and the clubface tends to close, delofting the face; increase the angle and it falls open, adding loft.

4. Lead with your chest

Release the clubhead through body rotation, not with your hands. Feel your chest turn through, leading your arms. Body releasing keeps the hands quiet.

The club decelerates into impact, causing erratic striking.

 Keep your weight on your front foot to promote a downward strike, and shorten your backswing.

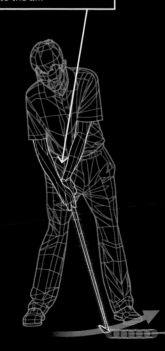

Leave it to the club
Don't let your hands flick at the ball to try to help it into the air.

Common fault
In a poor pitching action the golfer tries to help the ball into the air. By throwing the hands underneath the ball, to add loft to the club, you'll just end up catching the ball above the equator. Another problem arises if you leave too much weight on your right side: the club overtakes your hands and you could hit the ground heavy before the ball.

Poor pitching results from the club decelerating into impact. This happens when the backswing is too long, causing you to back off the shot for fear of overshooting. To stop the fat or thin pitch shot, favour your forward foot for weight at address and throughout the swing. Keeping your body steady will help the club deliver a downward blow.

The second point is to hinge your wrists halfway back, so the shaft forms a 90-degree angle with your forearm. Maintain this hinge position throughout the swing.

The final key is to make sure you make a full followthrough. If you stop your through-swing too short, you will constantly come up short.

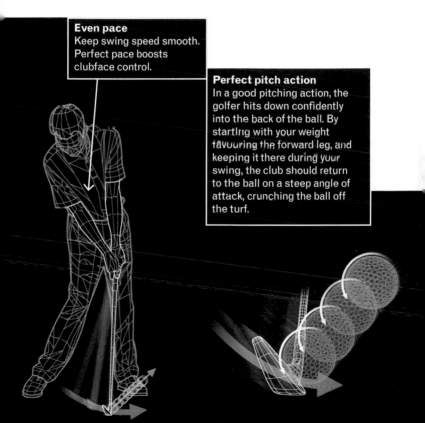

Even pace
Keep swing speed smooth. Perfect pace boosts clubface control.

Perfect pitch action
In a good pitching action, the golfer hits down confidently into the back of the ball. By starting with your weight favouring the forward leg, and keeping it there during your swing, the club should return to the ball on a steep angle of attack, crunching the ball off the turf.

Arms and body get out of sync, causing poor pitching control.

 Practise with a towel between your upper arms and body.

1. Simplify the set-up

Adopt a relaxed set-up position. The arms should stay close into your sides. Pop a golf towel underneath and squeeze it against the body slightly so it doesn't drop.

Straight and narrow
Narrow the stance a touch and turn your left foot out. This will make it easier to turn the shoulders.

2. Maintain the triangle

The backswing should feel compact, with everything turning in unison. Gain the right feeling by making sure the towel stays tucked under your arms. It ensures you maintain a perfect triangle between your arms and body, promoting a feeling of togetherness and control.

Arms stay close to body
Keep the backswing short and compact by turning the shoulders and hips in unison. Don't let the towel drop.

3. Mirror the backswing

Again, make sure you keep the towel tucked under your arms. This will help the arms to stay close into the body as you strike the ball into the through-swing. Finish with your club pointing at the target for pinpoint accuracy.

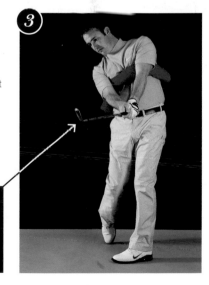

Stay compact throughout
Do not allow the arms to collapse as you swing through, but keep them close to your body. This aids a controlled execution.

You are faced with a nerve-shredding feel shot over water.

 Practise with a football to put your bigger muscles in control.

Water can be a psychological killer. You fear the wet stuff, and react to those fears by making a jerky, awkward swing. Most of the time your small muscles in the hands and arms are to blame for the ball splashing into trouble.

In a nervy swing, the wrists break down and the club hits the ground before the ball. To stop this happening you need to train the big body muscles to swing the club. A football can help.

Fear factor
Water hazards can spark nerves that lead to a 'handsy' nervous swing.

1. Adopt your stance

Adopt your normal golf posture, tilting forwards from the hips with a slight knee flex. Stretch your arms straight out in front of you and hold the football in your hands, so that you grip both sides of the ball.

2. Full shoulder turn

Swing the ball back, turning your left shoulder under your chin. The weight of the ball will help you to make a full shoulder turn, and by holding it in your hands the wrists won't be able to hinge.

3. Through impact

Return the ball through impact, rotating it by allowing your forearms to roll over while transferring weight to your left side. Register the feeling of the body muscles being in control, the hands quiet.

You need height, but your ball is on a downslope.

Swing down the slope and release the clubface under the ball.

The downhill lob shot is one of golf's toughest. Not only are you fighting a severe slope – you are also battling against a tough pin position on the near edge of the green. The only way to pull this off is to take the aerial route and flop the ball high, so that it lands softly. This is a high-risk shot that can't be mastered without practice; but it's worth the effort.

Head down
It is very easy to lift up on this shot and lose your balance as the slope tips you forwards. To counter-balance the forces of gravity keep your knees extra flexed and your eyes down, focusing on the grass until after the ball has been struck.

Hands release
In order for the club to slide underneath the ball, the hands must release the club so that the clubface points up towards the sky as you swing through.

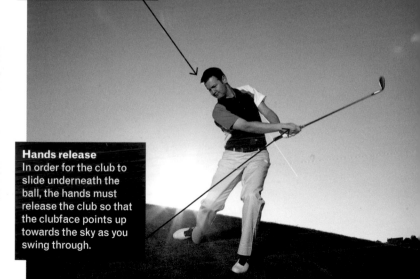

1. **Widen your base**

You need to ensure you have a stable footing, so widen your stance and exaggerate the knee flex. Let your weight favour the slope (lower leg) – don't try to fight it. Aim a little left.

2. **Pick up steeply**

Take the most lofted club in your bag, open the clubface and grip down. Pick the club up short and steep, with plenty of wrist hinge, to prevent it snagging on the bank.

3. **Swing down the slope**

With the clubface wide open, it should slide under the ball as it glides down the slope. Let the club travel forwards towards the pin. But the key to this shot is to commit to playing it with conviction.

You have no green to work with – and there's a trap in your way.

Set-up like a trap shot, hold the face open ... and swing with confidence.

Sharp-shooting American Phil Mickelson is king of the flop shot. His magical lob sends the ball soaring into the air with little forward carry and quick stop on the green. This do-or-die shot requires confidence and total commitment to execute, but is always a crowd-pleaser as it lands softly by the pin. Once mastered, this shot is guaranteed to impress your friends.

Hold it off
The clubface should stay wide open, pointing at the sky, as you swing through.

1. Open fire

Imagine you are playing a soft splash shot from the sand. Aim your feet, knees, hips and shoulders left of the target and lie the clubface wide open.

2. Steeper back

Pick the clubhead up steeply in your backswing, using plenty of wrist hinge. This will make it easier for you to slide the club across and under the ball.

3. Flip through

Make a full, smooth though-swing, allowing your hands to 'release' at impact, so that the clubhead flips underneath the ball, sending it upwards.

You have a lot of green to cover to reach the pin.

 Use low loft and a shoulder pendulum motion to keep the ball low and running.

When it comes to greenside touch shots there's one golden rule – always get the ball running out as soon as possible. The sooner the ball is running on the green the less chance of it getting an awkward bounce that

knocks it off-line. In fact, the technique is very similar to a putt – simply rock the club back and forth in a pendulum from the shoulders. You can use any club to play it; the further away the pin is, the less lofted the club should be.

Glove badge to the target
You must keep your wrists firm to play this shot successfully. Keep the back of the gloved hand facing the target as you swing through.

Keep your lower body quiet
Your lower half must support you as you swing the arms back and through in a rocking action from the shoulders.

1. Simplify your set-up

There should be very little lower body movement here. Narrow your stance, turn the left toe out towards the target slightly and move the ball back to inside your right foot. Grip down the club to gain control

2. Pick a landing spot

To help you judge the slopes, walk on to the green and look from the pin back to the ball. Look from the side too. You should pick a flat area where you want the ball to land.

3. Rock back

The technique is very similar to a putt; you want to take the hands out of the action. Rock the club back from the shoulders like a pendulum, but don't let the clubhead reach waist height.

4. Keep a firm left wrist

The only way you can mess up this shot is by letting the wrists interfere. Grip a little tighter and keep the back of your upper hand facing the target as you strike the ball.

You keep chunking chip shots (1).

 Use two household objects to help take the hands out of the stroke.

The main reason golfers struggle to hit their chips crisply is because their hands interfere with the action. If the hands flick underneath the ball, to try to help it up into the air, the club gets cast into the ground behind the ball and you hit the turf. Here are two simple training aids that can help.

1. Miss the magazine
The key is to hit down into the back of the ball, catching it cleanly before the turf. To get this descending blow, pop an object like a magazine a few inches behind the ball. Miss the mag, strike the ball.

2. Don't let the hanger hinge
To take your hands out of the action, grip the club against the straight edge of a hanger and practise swinging. Feel the hanger pressing against the underside of your left forearm throughout.

You keep chunking chip shots (2).

Find an old shaft and use it to help pacify 'flicky' wrists.

Poor chippers usually have a very wristy action. This makes the ball strike unpredictable. To train a wrist-free stroke, take a golf shaft and push it into the small hole in the butt end of the club. This will act as a barrier to flicky wrists.

Why do the wrists flick?
With weight too far back in the stance, the hands will release the club too early, hitting the ground heavy behind the ball.

Resist the release
Let weight favour the front foot. Keep hands ahead of the ball, so the extra shaft rests away from your body. Rock the club from the shoulders, like a putter.

Left hand leads
Keep the hands quiet by making sure the back of your left wrist stays flat and pointing at your target. If the hands break down, the shaft will hit your side.

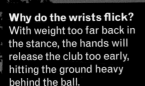

You've begun to shank your touch shots round the green.

 Rotate forearms to square the face.

One of the most common causes of a shank is a lack of forearm rotation. This simple one-arm drill will fix that.

Hands don't release
The hands return to impact too far ahead of the ball, the back of the left wrist is facing the sky and hasn't rotated, and the clubhead lags behind, wide open in relation to the target.

One-arm swing
Swinging the club in your right hand only will force the arm to rotate. Use this drill a few times and then transfer the correct sensation back to your golf swing.

Your approach has rolled up against the cut of the fringe.

 Pick a wedge, make a putting stroke and blade the ball forwards.

The belly wedge is often the only shot that will work effectively when your ball comes to rest up against the fringe of the green. With fluffy grass behind the ball, it is awkward to get a putter to strike it low enough to get it rolling. But attempt the same technique with the leading edge of a wedge and the ball can roll smoothly.

1. Hover halfway
To 'blade' the ball you must hover the straight leading edge of the club halfway up the ball, aiming to strike its equator.

2. Putt it
The technique is identical to that you'd use if you were playing a putt. Grip at the bottom of the grip, with a nice wide putting stance, and then simply rock the shoulders back and through, with no wrist action.

From the Sand

Stacks of simple bunker keys that
will bolster your strategy, technique
and confidence from traps

You struggle to make solid contact from fairway bunkers.

 Forget trying to nip it clean; set-up for a downward strike that takes a sand divot after the ball.

Finding your ball sat proudly on a bed of firm fairway sand 150 yards or more from the pin may not, at first glance, seem like a daunting prospect. It may seem easy to get greedy and go for the green, but this shot takes skill and practice. The trick is to learn to strike the ball first and the sand second.

Maintain tension: grip tighter to help
The fairway bunker shot is one of the few in golf where you can grip the club fairly tightly. A bit of tension in the arms will restrict wrist hinge to help catch the ball clean.

The right order: ball then sand
The club must strike just below the equator of the ball before making contact with the sand in order to flush your fairway bunker shot cleanly on to the green.

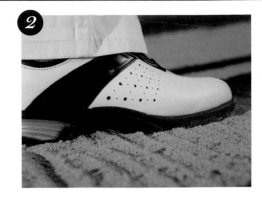

1. Correct ball position

To ensure you hit the ball first and not the sand, move the ball an inch further back in your stance than you would normally place it. Also grip down the club an inch to shorten it.

2. Place your feet

Unlike on a greenside bunker shot, don't dig your feet into the sand. Simply place them in position on top of the surface and give them a slight shuffle to ensure a stable footing.

3. Shorter backswing

The swing should be very controlled. Keep your backswing short, no more than a three-quarter swing, use a little less wrist hinge and keep a little tension in your forearms.

4. Strike the ball first

This is the opposite technique to a greenside bunker shot so will need practice. Try to strike a point just below the equator of the ball so you clip it cleanly off the top of the sand.

You're in sand but between a full swing and a standard splash shot, some 70 yards from the green.

 Play it like a normal pitch and take a fraction of sand.

The key to playing the long bunker shot well is to splash just the right amount of sand out with your ball. It takes patience and practice to get the strike right. The technique goes against many of the principles you put into play for the short splash shot out of sand. You'll need to trust this new method to make it work.

Long bunker shot
Take sand with this shot – but only a pinch just behind the ball.

1. Set-up as for a pitch shot

Play this shot exactly the same way you would play a pitch shot from outside the sand. Keep your stance and the clubface square to the flag – don't open them up.

2. Swing around the body

Concentrate on keeping your left arm close to your chest as you turn your back to the target. This will help you to sweep the club low around your body, rather than picking it up steeply.

3. Focus on the strike

Make a full swing and focus on striking a point just behind the ball in the sand. Make sure you accelerate into the sand and complete the followthrough so you finish balanced, facing the flag.

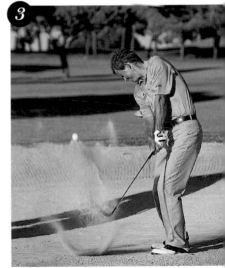

You struggle to take the right amount of sand, so are hitting long and short.

 Focus on swing length, the sand wedge's sole … and a banknote.

The first rule of bunker play is that you must hit the sand before you hit the ball. If you don't, you'll never get the ball out. A simple drill is to imagine a banknote resting underneath the ball. In order to hit the ball out, you must splash the entire note out with it. That means allowing the sand wedge to enter and exit the sand a couple of inches either side of the ball. You can even trace around a banknote in the sand when you practise and pop a ball in the centre to help you master this trick.

1. Basic set-up

Open the clubface of your sand wedge, grip softly, shuffle your feet down into the sand and open your stance so that your body aims a few feet left of the target, but your clubface aims at the pin.

2. Accelerate through

The key to splashing shots out of sand successfully is not to be afraid of hitting the sand. The club must splash through the sand aggressively into your finish.

Impact
Splash the sand, the ball and the banknote out of the bunker towards the target.

Basic swing
Make a three-quarter length backswing and through-swing keeping the leg action quiet.

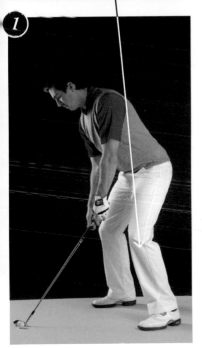

3

3. Vary the distance

The next skill you need to master is how to vary the distance you hit your sand shots. You should swing the club back three-quarters as shown and then practise varying the length of your followthrough. Try some, quarter, half and full finish positions.

Lower yourself
Exaggerate knee flex to lower your centre of gravity; keep this height to the finish.

4

4. Use the bounce

The bounce on the sole of the sand wedge stops the clubhead digging the sand. To do the same, position the ball opposite your left eye and let the shaft angle of your sand wedge lean back so that it points towards your belly button. From here, make sure that as you swing through, the right palm faces up towards the sky.

Finish high

Swing high so that your hands are higher than your shoulders in the finish to ensure maximum loft stays on the wedge.

You struggle to adapt your bunker technique to different sand firmness.

 Improve your understanding of how 'bounce' works on the sole of your sand wedge.

Hitting out of soft sand

When the sand is deep and soft, the club will dig in far easier, causing you to hit shots heavy. To counter this, go for a wedge with added bounce. As the sole of the club makes contact with the sand it should skim across the top surface layer, carrying the ball out with it. Remember: always accelerate through the sand and finish your swing. If the club digs and stays in the sand, chances are your ball will stay in the sand too.

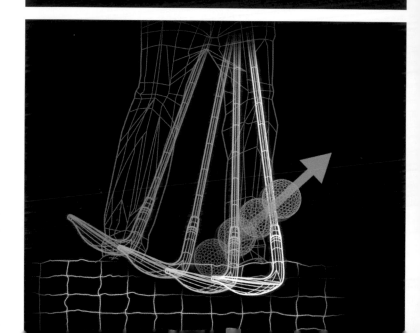

All golfers need to play out of soft, fluffy sand and hard, wet sand. For success from both lies you need to understand how the 'bounce' on your sand wedge works. The bounce of the wedge is the bulging area on the bottom, which allows the club to slide through the sand rather than digging in. The more you open the clubface, the more bounce you'll apply. From soft sand you need to slide under the ball, skimming the surface layer of the sand. Open the clubface wide to add bounce and prevent it digging in.

The opposite applies from wet sand. You don't want the face open because the added bounce causes the club to skip off the firm surface, leading to a thin shot. Instead, square the face up to reduce the bounce.

Hitting out of hard sand
When the sand is firm and compact, the club will naturally bounce off the surface rather than dig in. In these conditions it is easy to thin your shots long over the back of the green. To help prevent this happening, use a wedge that has less bounce, so that the leading edge of the club can dig into the sand, popping the ball up and out. Remember: even if the sand is compacted, you must hit into it before striking the ball.

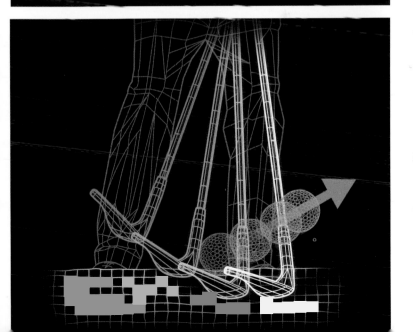

Your ball has plugged in a greenside trap. Just half the ball is visible.

 Let your handicap govern your approach – and your strategy.

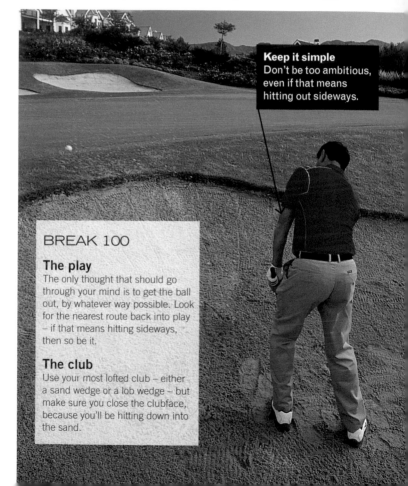

Keep it simple
Don't be too ambitious, even if that means hitting out sideways.

BREAK 100

The play
The only thought that should go through your mind is to get the ball out, by whatever way possible. Look for the nearest route back into play – if that means hitting sideways, then so be it.

The club
Use your most lofted club – either a sand wedge or a lob wedge – but make sure you close the clubface, because you'll be hitting down into the sand.

1. Safely does it

When you reach the ball, check to see how close it has plugged to the lip. If it's under the lip then look at the ground to the sides of the bunker and aim to play out to the side that offers the best chance of a two-putt.

2. Close the clubface

Turn the toe of the club inwards and then take your grip. You should still hover the club behind the back of the ball, but aim to hit down steeply into the sand. By closing the clubface the club will drive down far easier into the sand.

3. Pick the club up steeply

Your backswing should be short and steep. Use plenty of wrist hinge to raise the club up, so that it points straight up at the sky. From here, you just need to drive the clubhead down into the sand. Be positive, don't quit on it and the ball will pop out.

BREAK 90

The play

Attacking the pin is not really the sensible option for you. Instead, look for the widest part of the green and aim to splash the ball out to this point.

The club

A sand wedge is the only option if you are going to attempt to play forwards over the lip.

1. The sensible play

Don't get greedy and try to play for the pin. The sensible play is to aim for where the lip carry is less steep; you'll have a greater margin for error.

2. Square the club

You don't need to open or close the clubface; its natural loft will do the job. Focus on hitting the sand just behind the ball as you would for a normal shot.

3. Short is better

You must take a lot of sand to get the ball out, so your followthrough will be stunted. Don't worry; just ensure the club drives aggressively beneath the ball.

BREAK 80

The play
This is a specialist technique that should only be attempted if you have a high skill level. You'll be aiming straight at the pin, and hitting down hard into the sand.

The club
You definitely need plenty of loft on your club to play this shot, so a sand wedge – or even better a lob wedge – is essential.

1. Go for the pin
The power that goes into this shot should mean the ball pops out no matter what direction you hit it in. It may seem bold but aiming for the pin is the right move.

2. Open the club
You need maximum loft to play this shot well, so open the clubface wide before you take your grip. Then hover the club at the point you want it to enter the sand.

3. Hit and recoil
The harder you can hit down into the sand the better. As soon as you hit it, feel the club recoiling back towards you. This makes it bounce through the sand, helping the ball to pop up high and land softly.

Your ball is lying well, but under the lip. You need height fast.

 Open the face and play with aggression and commitment.

You don't need Mickelsonesque skills to advance the ball from under the lip – just a couple of pointers, some clubhead speed and the belief that you can get the job done.

Keep it under control

The faster you swing, the more effective this shot will be. But remember that your swing must stay under control. Make sure you shuffle your feet down into the sand, to give yourself a firm base around which you can generate that power.

Check the lie
If the ball is not sitting up on the sand then it's not sensible to try this shot.

1. Clubface wide open
You need maximum height on this shot if you're going to splash your ball out. Open the club wide so that a tee placed on it would point straight up at the sky.

2. Set the wrists early
Your backswing should be short and steep with maximum wrist hinge. Pick the club up vertically and drive down into the sand, blasting the ball out.

3. Speed is essential
You need maximum forward momentum on the clubhead to get the ball out. Don't be afraid to blast the club into the sand and through into the lip.

Your ball is lying in wet, sodden sand but there's not enough standing water for a drop.

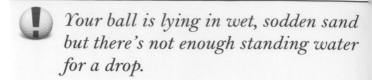 Square the face and swing with a short, punchy action.

Be brave
Don't be afraid of really hitting down hard into the sand. A positive attack will guarantee your ball pops out of the wet sand and on to the green.

Address
Keep your clubface square at address and hover it above the point you want to enter the sand.

Backswing
Your backswing should be short; simply pick the club up steeply, then drive into the sand.

1. Keep the clubface square

Unlike a traditional bunker shot where you open the clubface of your sand wedge, keep it square to help the club dig into the sand.

2. Hit down to pop the ball out

The technique from wet sand requires a steep descending blow into the back of the ball. Keep your weight on the left side to help the club follow a straight-up, straight-down path.

3. Swing short to long

It is very easy for all the wet sand to absorb the energy of the shot. Keeping your backswing short will ensure you strike down and through the wet sand, without quitting.

Followthrough
Aim to reach a full followthrough position. This prevents the club quitting as it enters the sand.

Your ball hasn't plugged but, as often happens, it's managed to nestle.

 Don't hit the ball any harder, but steepen your angle of attack.

More often than not, the ball manages to find some rake groove or little hollow that makes a trap shot seem a very different proposition. Many golfers resort to a thrash at the sand. But you don't have to; it's possible to play a high controlled shot from a cuppy trap lie. The trick is to swing steeply into the ball while keeping loft on the clubface. Follow these steps.

Steep action: hit down to the ball
You need to hinge your wrists early in your backswing to get that all-important downward angle of attack at impact.

Under the ball: fly high, land soft
Feel you are throwing your right hand under the ball at impact; this will help the club's 'bounce' to glide through the sand.

1. Forward ball position

Keep the ball forwards in your stance – just inside your left instep. Add loft to the clubface too; it goes against the normal squaring-up advice, but you want height.

2. Shift weight forwards

Feel like you have perhaps 60 per cent of your weight on your front foot. The shot you're going to play requires a steep backswing – weight forwards encourages it.

3. Set your wrists early

Make a brisk and purposeful wrist hinge early in the backswing. This, coupled with your front foot weight, sets up a sharp action and a steep angle of attack.

4. Use that bounce

Release the clubhead into the sand by throwing your right hand under the ball. Feel the clubface overtake your hands, and even the ball. This allows the club's bounce to work.

Great Escapes

Effective solutions for getting out of golf's trickiest situations – and keeping a disaster off your scorecard

Your ball is sitting down in the semi-rough, and you still need distance.

 Pick your utility club; make a crisp swing with a descending strike.

Set-up to hit down
Your only chance of a clean strike is to strike down on the ball. Pre-set this by playing the ball centrally in your stance, and by positioning your hands just ahead of the clubface. The hybrid has plenty of loft to get the ball up.

Early wrist hinge
With this lie you'll need to dig a little. So set those wrists early in your backswing to create the steeper swing shape and later hit that will help the hybrid's face strike down.

Left shoulder
Turn until your left shoulder is above the inside of your right heel. This ensures you transfer your weight on to the right side. Although you're priming a downward blow, you still need a little width.

Top hand pressure
The heel/hosel end of the face meets more resistance from a tangly lie than the toe area. That can cause the clubface to close, and your ball to dive left. Guard against this by gripping more tightly with your top hand.

Short followthrough
Keep your action crisp and punchy by committing to a shortish followthrough. Your hands should finish at about head height and in front of your body.

Your ball has stayed dry but left you with this horror stance on the edge of a water hazard.

 Grip well down the shaft, and shallow your swing plane.

You might think you've made a lucky escape if you ball comes up just short of water. But if it is lying beyond the coloured stakes you're technically in the hazard, a that means you can't groun your club without incurring a penalty stroke. Make the most of your good fortune b following these three simple tips – grip down, hover the club above the grass and swing flat around your body

Out of trouble
Grip down to shorten the shaft and hover the clubhead above the grass.

1. Grip down for control
Because the ball is raised above your feet, you need to grip down to the bottom of the handle to shorten the length of the shaft. This will help guard against the club digging into the ground before impact.

2. Open and hover
You need maximum loft to escape this tough lie, so lie the clubface wide open and then take your grip. Be careful not to ground your club as you settle on the bank. Hover it behind the ball.

3. Swing around the body
You need a flat, rounded swing to play this shot well. Practise making rounded swings at waist height, then transfer this feeling to the bank. The shot puts right-to-left spin on the ball, so aim well right of trouble.

Winter golf means a variety of tricky lies in long, wet, lush grass.

Learn to read the lie before establishing your best escape route.

Grass grows with you
If your ball finishes on top of rough grass, and the grass is pointing towards your target, then you need to beware of catching a flier.

1. Clean strike

You need to play this shot like a fairway bunker, and aim to strike the ball cleanly. Take one club less, and move the ball position further forward towards your left hee

2. Strong position

Focus on keeping a stable lower half, to help keep your upper body height as you strike th ball and prevent the club catching the grass before your ball.

Plugged lie
You need to drive the ball out of a plugged lie by hitting down steeply into the grass surrounding it; be prepared to take a duvet-style divot.

1. Ball back, hands ahead
Use the same technique that you'd need to get out of a divot. Move the ball back to opposite your right foot and shift your hands ahead of the ball.

2. Pick the club up
Pick the club up steeply in the backswing. Accentuate wrist hinge and keep the weight on your left side.

3. Make a big divot
Drive your hips forwards towards the target so that the club returns to the back of the ball on a steep descent.

Grass grows against you
When the ball nestles down into the rough and the blades of grass are growing against the ball, the club can easily get caught up and turn over.

1. Take control
Strengthen your grip (thumbs to the right for right-handers) to help keep control of a clubhead that will get snagged up in the grass as it strikes the ball.

2. On target
Keep your glove badge (back of the left wrist or watch) pointing towards the target as you strike the ball. This will help to prevent the clubface from closing.

Ball buried in rough
When the ball nestles down into deep grass, you have to dig. Move the ball position well back in your stance to ensure you hit down. Open the clubface of your wedge slightly to help the club cut through the grass.

1. Wrist action

Use plenty of wrist hinge to pick the club up steeply towards the sky in your backswing. This primes a steep attack.

2. Impact

Drive down positively into the back of the ball. The face may want to close; your open face at set-up should allow for that.

Your ball is lying well, but there's a huge chunk of mud on it – and the rules won't let you clean and replace.

 The mud will make the ball veer left or right – so aim off to allow.

There's no exact science to guarantee how the ball will fly, but there are some rules of thumb that should help minimize your misfortune:

1. Mud fact
Nine times out of ten the ball will veer in the direction of the mud. So if it's on the right side of the ball it will slice, and if it's on the left it will hook.

2. Aim off
Take an extra club and aim further left than normal – or right if the mud's on the other side.

3. Play confidently
The rest is in the lap of the gods. Forget about the mud and commit to making a good strike.

Your ball has rolled to the foot of a tree, completely blocking your stance.

 Try the left-handed back-hander.

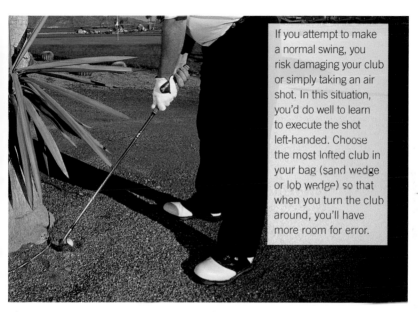

If you attempt to make a normal swing, you risk damaging your club or simply taking an air shot. In this situation, you'd do well to learn to execute the shot left-handed. Choose the most lofted club in your bag (sand wedge or lob wedge) so that when you turn the club around, you'll have more room for error.

1. Back-hander
Turn your sand wedge upside down and grip it back to front, with your left hand low and your right hand high.

2. Prepare the ground
You'll need to remain very still as you swing, so check your stance is solid, with your weight just favouring your front foot.

3. Keep it simple
Don't try to be too clever with this shot. Take the club straight back and through with very little wrist action, like a left-handed putt.

4. Stay still
Avoid lateral movement and weight shift. You need serious precision here, so the more stable you can stay, the better your chances of success.

Your ball is sitting on loose debris.

 Set-up to make a short punchy swing, your hands leading the club through impact.

Strike order
You need to strike the ball before the needles from this lie.

One false step here could cause the ball to move without you striking it – and that means a penalty shot. So the first tip is to tread carefully. Once you're set-up to strike the ball, the next biggest problem to avoid is fatting the shot completely. To stop the debris disintegrating beneath your club, you'll need to play a low punch shot. Here's how:

1. Use a long iron

It would be easy to grab your pitching wedge to chip out of the trees back into play, but doing so could be disastrous. There's too much loft on a short iron – not only will the club dig into the debris, it will pop the ball up too high into the air, bringing low, hanging branches into play. Choose a long iron instead.

2. Ball back, grip down

The key to playing this shot well is to strike the ball first, before the debris, with a descending blow. Position the ball opposite your back foot and grip down the shaft for control. You want to keep the swing short but controlled, punching the ball out low, under the branches of the trees, back into play.

3. Accelerate through

The only way you'll recover from this situation is by using a positive attack. Your backswing will probably be restricted, but make sure you accelerate through. Try to keep your hands ahead of the clubface to ensure minimum loft on the club as it strikes the ball. It should shoot out low and running.

You're in shallow water, but the top of the ball breaks the surface.

 Take a lofted club, make a steep backswing, and drive down.

If half the ball breaks the surface of the water, then the shot described above is perfectly achievable to attempt. To practise it, place your ball no more than two feet from the bank of the water hazard. Take your shoes and socks off and step into the hazard, making sure your feet are firmly grounded. Bend your knees and lean back into the hazard. Take your most lofted club and grip down for extra control. Pick the club up steeply and drive down into the water.

1. Assess the lie
Make sure at least half your ball is showing above the water. If any less than half is visible you can forget it!

2. Do or die
Lean back to help launch the ball up and out. Drive down behind the ball into the drink, almost like a bunker shot.

Your ball is lying cleanly but under a bush, stopping a regular stance.

 Drop to your knees and aim to strike the equator of the ball.

Save yourself a penalty shot by dropping down on to your knees and swinging a club around your body at waist height, like you would a baseball bat. With a bit of practice this new skill could save you many shots.

1. On your knees
Kneel down and look at the branches. If they are lower than two feet from the ground, your ball won't come out. If you can see a sizeable gap, grip at the very bottom of the handle of a mid-iron, and push your hands ahead of the ball.

2. Baseball swing
Practise this by holding a club at waist height and swinging it like a baseball bat. Now transfer this feeling to the kneeling position. Try to keep the club low to the ground in the backswing and sweep it through around your body.

3. Middle hit
You can easily catch the ground before the ball. Prevent this by focusing on striking halfway up the ball, on its equator. Let your hands lead the club through; this should prevent it driving into the ground.

4

 Your ball is lying in six-inch greenside rough.

 Favour your left side and drive down and through.

The key to playing this shot with finesse is to select the most lofted club in your bag (sand wedge or lob wedge), settle yourself into the grass with the weight favouring your left side, and then to drive down powerfully into the grass behind your ball.

Most golfers only ever practise hitting balls off a perfect lie, so make a point of practising from difficult conditions like this. Do so and tricky shots will become second nature.

1. Lean towards the green

You'll need to use your most lofted club. Set-up with a wide stance, your weight favouring the left side. Lean towards the green to encourage a steeper angle of attack. Exaggerate knee flex to lower your centre of gravity – this will make it easier for the club to drive through the grass.

2. Pick the club up steeply

Grip at the bottom of the handle to shorten the shaft and make the club more controllable. Also tighten your hold on the club, as this will prevent the clubhead twisting as it enters the grass. Now pick the club up steeply into the air and hinge your wrists, so that the butt end of the club points straight down at the ball.

3. Drive through the grass

Accelerate into the back of the ball so the club drives through the grass. Entering the grass with speed also helps the clubhead to cut through the rough. Don't worry if the grass restricts your followthrough – just focus on getting your ball out into play.

Your ball has missed the greenside trap but found the slope near it.

Play the ball closer to your higher foot to minimize the slope's effect.

Uphill slope

Playing off an uphill slope is like teeing off from a launch pad. Getting the ball airborne is easy – you have to learn how to control where it lands.

Weight shift
The hardest thing to do on an upslope is get your weight forwards through the ball. If your weight stays back on the right side, you'll flip your hands over and hit a hook. Beat this by driving your weight forwards to your front foot as you swing through, holding the clubface square to the target.

1. Check your angles
Set your shoulders and hips on the same angle as the upslope by leaning back, away from the target. This helps the club return to the ball on the same, sweeping arc as for a level lie. Use two clubs to check shoulder your angle.

2. On the up
Always play the ball closer to your front foot on an upslope. This will encourage you to catch the ball cleanly.

Downhill slope

Playing off a downhill slope is a much harder challenge. The trick is not to fight the slope, but to blend with the terrain and keep your balance.

Stay put
You're trying to hit the ball into the air from a severe downslope. Your brain is telling you that you must try and scoop it into the air. That would signal disaster. Instead, keep your eyes glued to the spot where the ball was for a full second after impact. That will ensure your body stays down through the hitting area.

1. Check your angles

Drop your left shoulder until your backbone is at right angles to the slope; use a couple of clubs to check that your shoulders are level with the ground. Leaning forwards promotes a downward angle of attack, helping you to strike the ball cleanly.

2. Downward swing

Play the ball closer to your back foot than your front. The steeper the slope, the further back you should move the ball. This will help you catch the ball on the club's swooping, downward swing arc.

Putting

Putting fears banished – from three-putting to lipping out on shorties – courtesy of the flatstick experts

Your putting is sabotaged by too much hand manipulation during the stroke.

 Grip the putter in your palms to calm your hands.

A successful putting grip keeps the hands quiet and in a square position throughout the stroke – which means they are parallel to each other and to the clubface. Achieve this and you reduce the chance of manipulating the face to point away from your target. The classic reverse overlap grip is often acknowledged by coaches to be the most successful way of holding the putter. Follow these four simple steps to form it – and keep those hands quiet.

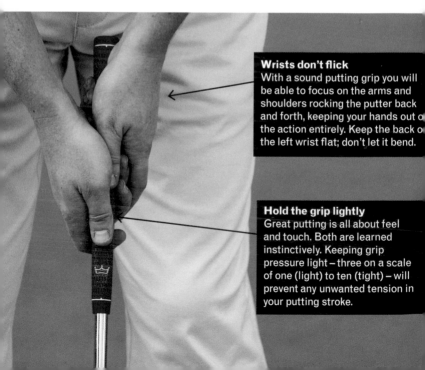

Wrists don't flick
With a sound putting grip you will be able to focus on the arms and shoulders rocking the putter back and forth, keeping your hands out of the action entirely. Keep the back of the left wrist flat; don't let it bend.

Hold the grip lightly
Great putting is all about feel and touch. Both are learned instinctively. Keeping grip pressure light – three on a scale of one (light) to ten (tight) – will prevent any unwanted tension in your putting stroke.

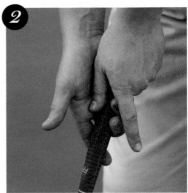

1. Grip sits in the lifeline

Rest the putter along the lifeline of your left hand, so it runs from the corner of your wrist, across the fleshy pad of your hand to the middle socket of your index finger. Close the hand around that line.

2. Introduce the right hand

Add the right hand to the other side of the grip, but this time place the putter grip slightly lower in the palm of your hand, so it rests more in your right-hand fingers.

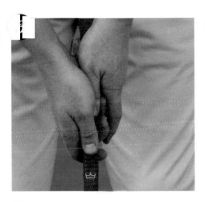

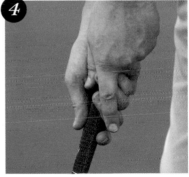

3. Overlap the hands

Join the hands and overlap them so they work as one unit. Lift the right hand and allow the left-hand thumb to sit in the crease of your right hand.

4. Add a trigger finger

Place the index finger of your left hand so that it overlaps and rests across the last three fingers of the right hand, pointing down the shaft of the putter.

You make a loopy stroke, which promotes inconsistency.

Square the putter blade at set-up.

Poor aim

Many poor putters start by aiming the putter incorrectly. To compensate for the misalignment, the putter is then taken away on an inside path towards the toes. The player rectifies this by looping the putter back high and across the target line. The putterface is held open as it strikes the ball, imparting sidespin that causes the ball to slice and miss the hole. Improve the aim of the blade and the path of the stroke.

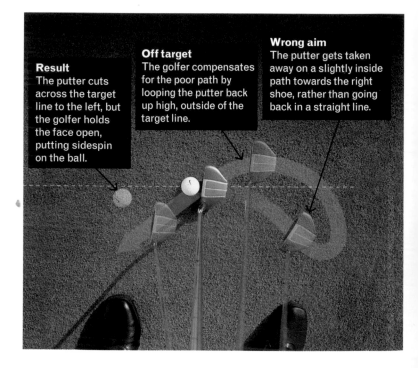

Result
The putter cuts across the target line to the left, but the golfer holds the face open, putting sidespin on the ball.

Off target
The golfer compensates for the poor path by looping the putter back up high, outside of the target line.

Wrong aim
The putter gets taken away on a slightly inside path towards the right shoe, rather than going back in a straight line.

Straight back and through

For all putts within 15ft of the hole, the putter should follow an imaginary line to the hole, straight back and straight through. The easiest way to practise this is to lie two clubs on the ground as train tracks and putt in between them. Keep the clubs close together – you want less than an inch either side of the putter to make the challenge tough. Rock the shoulders to create the pendulum action.

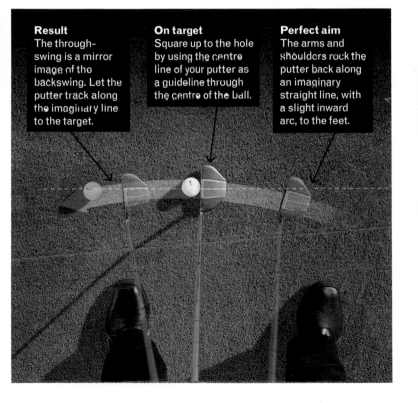

Result
The through-swing is a mirror image of the backswing. Let the putter track along the imaginary line to the target.

On target
Square up to the hole by using the centre line of your putter as a guideline through the centre of the ball.

Perfect aim
The arms and shoulders rock the putter back along an imaginary straight line, with a slight inward arc, to the feet.

The ball bobbles off the putter's face, kicking off-line.

Use ball position to encourage an upward brush on the ball.

The correct position for the ball in your stance is two inches ahead of your sternum. You can check this by resting the grip end of your putter against the centre of your chest. The shaft will point down at the ground. Use this as a reference point to show you the lowest point in your putting stroke where the putter will strike the ground. The ball should then be positioned two inches ahead of this point in your stance to ensure that you strike it on the upstroke, imparting topspin that will give you a truer run out across the green.

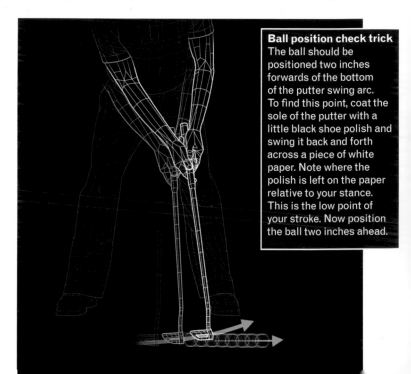

Ball position check trick
The ball should be positioned two inches forwards of the bottom of the putter swing arc. To find this point, coat the sole of the putter with a little black shoe polish and swing it back and forth across a piece of white paper. Note where the polish is left on the paper relative to your stance. This is the low point of your stroke. Now position the ball two inches ahead.

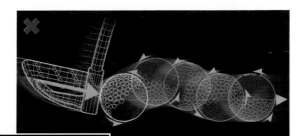

Bumpy roll
When the ball jumps excessively on leaving the putterface it's a sign that you have the ball positioned too far back in your stance. The putter is striking the ball at the low point of your stroke, imparting too much backspin and sending it spiralling across the green.

Smooth roll
With the ball positioned correctly in your stance you will be able to strike it on the upstroke, imparting topspin that will send it rolling smoothly across the green. Remember to keep your swing tempo even and rock the putter back and forth from the shoulders without using the hands.

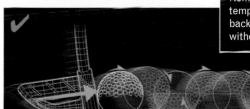

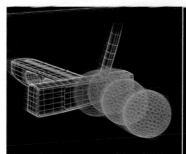

Shaft leans forwards
To help put a smoother roll on the ball, when you take your set-up position lean the shaft of the putter slightly forwards and then take your grip. Coupled with the correct ball position this forward hand start position will mean that you develop a glancing upward strike as you hit the ball on the upstroke, maximizing your smooth ball roll.

The putterface is not square at impact.

 Roll a pencil towards your target.

An easy drill to train a square face is to pop a pencil on the green in place of your golf ball. Place the pencil at right-angles to the hole and address it as you would a ball. Now strike the pencil. If you hit it pure, it should run out straight towards the hole; a non-square face will make it curve off sideways.

Pencil practice
Put a pencil or piece of lightweight tubing on the green, at right-angles to the hole, in place of the golf ball. The aim is to strike the pencil with a square putterface, so that it rolls out straight towards the hole.

You struggle to strike the ball out of your putter's sweet-spot.

 Coat the face in sunscreen, hit some putts and assess the marks.

To put a smooth, straight roll on the ball you'll need to strike your putts out of the sweet-spot, in the centre of the putterface. If you are striking from the heel or the toe, it can twist the blade open or closed and affect your success. Use sunscreen to find out if mishits are your problem.

Central strike
The perfect strike mark is in the centre of the putterface. This is a clear indication that you have hit your putt straight towards your intended target.

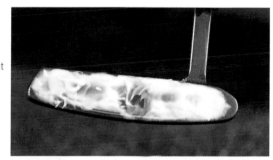

Toe mark
If your putts are struck out of the toe of the putter then you'll send putts right of the hole. This happens when the putter is swung out to the right, instead of straight towards the hole.

Heel mark
If you strike your putts close to the heel then you'll either pull putts left or slice them with left-to-right sidespin. The cause is often simply lifting your head too soon, to see if your putt has dropped.

Your touch from long range is poor, causing you to three-putt greens.

Improve your striking by working on the rhythm of the stroke.

Most amateurs struggle to putt close from long range due to erratic striking. Finding the putter's sweet-spot is essential if you are to build feel and consistency – and as the stroke gets longer, your mission gets harder. But you can improve your striking by making your set-up more solid, and by adding rhythm. Follow these four tips and watch how your touch improves.

Right set-up
Stability is key. Flex and brace your legs for a solid stance to avoid swaying. Keep your eyes over the ball so you have a clearer picture of its path to the hole.

Long shot
Erratic striking makes it really difficult to get consistency on long putts. Keep the butt of the putter pointing to your navel to promote clean contact and get your ball close.

1. Form a stable base

Start from a stable base by flexing and bracing your legs. The stroke can get quite lengthy on long putts; a solid stance kills swaying and boosts accurate striking.

2. Eyes over the ball

This doesn't just help you to form a more accurate picture of the ball's path to the hole – it also improves your chances of finding the putter's sweet-spot.

3. Light grip pressure

On long putts, the job of your hands is simply to transmit the power created by your swinging arms to the putter. Use a soft grip pressure to let them transmit without interference.

4. Belly button pointer

Keep the butt of the putter looking at your navel as you follow through. This keeps the arc of your stroke consistent and helps you release the putter more rhythmically.

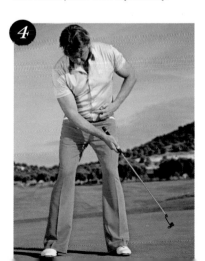

You have difficulty reading greens, costing you long range confidence.

 Build a tee-peg gateway to the putt's key breaking point.

Path finder
Use the tee-peg gateway to start your ball on the right line to the breaking point.

Looking for slopes is only part of the task; once you've identified the break across the surface, you need to find a sure-fire way of setting your ball rolling on the right path. Try this tee-peg gateway game when you practise and you'll become a much better lag putter.

1. Picture the path
Imagining a grid on the putting surface will help you picture how the slopes will make the ball curve as it rolls out. Draw a straight line on your ball and aim this in the direction you want your putt to start on.

2. Find the breaking point
Once you've got a general overview of the slopes, the next step is to find the peak of the slope – the final breaking point where the putt will run out straight down to the cup. Pop a tee in the ground to mark it.

3. Tee-peg gateway
Place two pegs 18 inches in front of the ball and two inches apart. Line the ball up to your breaking point in the distance, then putt through the pegs to start it on the right path.

You are putting on bumpy and inconsistent mid-winter greens.

 Strike the putt with topspin to help the ball hug the ground.

In the ideal putt the ball never leaves the ground – because when it lands, it has a nasty tendency to kick off-line. If you can hone a stroke that imparts overspin on the ball, you'll stand a much better chance of keeping the ball on the deck.

Beat the bumps
Winter greens tend to kick the ball up into the air. Make three adjustments to your putting set-up and stroke to help the ball track truer to the ground.

1. Set-up
Shift the ball position forwards to a couple of inches inside your left foot, but keep your hands in line with the ball.

2. Hover the putter
Avoid striking the base of the ball, as it will bounce straight into the air. Instead, hover your putter and aim to strike its equator.

3. Through and up
Aim to swing the putter through and up towards the sky. This will add topspin, helping the ball to roll out more smoothly.

You are not holing enough putts from inside 10ft, putting pressure on your long game.

 Practise drills to improve stroke and strike for better holing out.

In this distance-driven game, one fact remains: the fastest way to lower your scores is to putt well. You only need to glance at the stats of the world's best players for validation of that – four of the top ten players are also among the top ten putters. Good scores come from good putting, and good putting is the result of good fundamentals. Get them right and you'll be laughing.

1. Point the pen

Keep your head steady throughout the stroke to ensure a consistent putter path and strike. A simple way to practise it is to pop a pen in your mouth and let it point at the floor. Now simply keep the pen pointing down as you rock the putter back and through.

2. Boost the stroke

Poor putters often have too much hand action. By letting the wrists break down and interfere, the putterhead twists off-line as it strikes the ball and you inevitably miss putts. You must learn to keep the wrists passive. Squeeze a rugby ball between your forearms to keep them locked together in a V-shape. Don't allow the wrists to break down as the rugby ball will move.

3. Improve your strike

The final factor necessary to hole more putts is a perfect strike. Challenge your accuracy by placing a golf ball either side of your putter and then putt without disturbing the balls. To heighten the sense of connection between your arms pop a couple of headcovers under your armpits and don't let them drop as you rock the putter back and forth.

Your putts always lip out.

 Roll the ball with topspin.

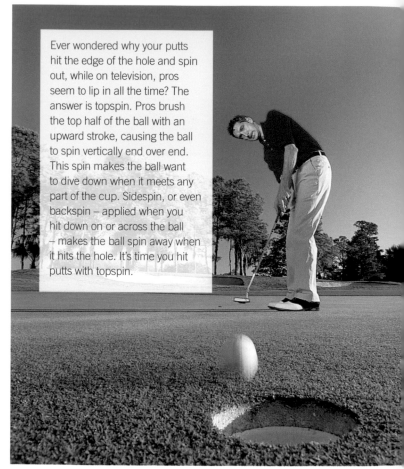

Ever wondered why your putts hit the edge of the hole and spin out, while on television, pros seem to lip in all the time? The answer is topspin. Pros brush the top half of the ball with an upward stroke, causing the ball to spin vertically end over end. This spin makes the ball want to dive down when it meets any part of the cup. Sidespin, or even backspin – applied when you hit down on or across the ball – makes the ball spin away when it hits the hole. It's time you hit putts with topspin.

1. Ball forwards

Position the ball opposite your left instep. This encourages an impact after the putter's arc has levelled out (around the middle of your stance), when it has begun to rise. This is perfect for that upward strike.

2. Take it back low

You can only hit up on the ball if the putterhead starts forwards from a low position, so imagine you are brushing the grass with the sole of the putter on the way back. Keep your hands and wrists quiet and your arms extended.

3. Scrape the top of the ball

In slow motion, practise moving the putter forwards and scraping the top of the ball with the bottom of the face. Keep focused and imagine the putter's face is going to clear the top of the ball, as if you are trying to take the paint off the top of the ball.

4. Refine your movement

As you practise, gradually increase the speed so you are putting ever so slightly faster each time. The ultimate aim is for you to be able to perform your normal-speed stroke while still catching the top half of the ball.

You have trouble lagging fast putts to the holeside.

 Strike the ball from the putter's toe.

Putting on super-slick greens can be nerve-racking; miss the first putt and you could face an even longer return. It's easy to become short and stabby with your stroke when you're fearful that the ball will run out of control past the hole. Fortunately, the solution couldn't be simpler: rather than striking the ball out of the centre of the putterhead, address it out of the toe. This will take a lot of the pace off the ball and allows you to concentrate on making a smooth stroke rocking from your shoulders like the pendulum of a clock.

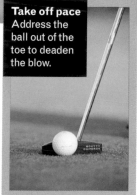

Take off pace Address the ball out of the toe to deaden the blow.

The Teaching Pros

Gareth Benson
Teaching professional at
the Astley Golf Range,
Manchester

Nick Bradley
Runs the Nick Bradley
School of Golf at the Barefoot
Resort, Myrtle Beach,
South Carolina

Jason Brant
Head professional at East
Berkshire Golf Club

Chris Brown
Head professional at
Westin Turnberry Golf
Resort, Ayrshire

Gary Casey
Senior teaching professional
at Thorpe Wood Golf Course,
Peterborough

Ian Clark
Director of Golf and
professional teacher at the
New Malden Golf Course

Nick Clemens
Director of Provision Golf,
Isle of Wight

Scott Cranfield
European Tour coach,
Director of Cranfield Golf
Academies and keynote
speaker for the PGA

Meyer du Toit
Head teaching professional,
Simola Golf Resort,
South Africa

Patrick Flynn
Professional coach at
the Woburn Golf Club,
Milton Keynes

Dan Friend
PGA professional and
Custom Fit Technician for
Acushnet at Brampton,
Cambridgeshire

Dan Frost
Head teaching professional
at CGA Sandown Park

Adrian Fryer
Head teaching professional
at Drivetime Range,
Warrington

Gareth Johnston
Assistant teaching
professional at East Berks
Golf Course

Phil Kenyon
Director of instruction for
Harold Swash Putting School

Robert Mitchell
CGA teaching professional
at Costa Ballena Golf
Resort, Spain

Stuart Morgan
Senior Assistant Golf
Professional at Prestwick
Golf Club

Lee Scarbrow
Head teaching professional
at John O'Gaunt Golf Club,
Bedfordshire

Derek Simpson
Senior Teaching Professional
at The Belfry, West Midlands

Mitchell Spearman
Director of Instruction at
Manhattan Woods Golf Club
in West Nyack, New York

Index